Facts About Honeybees

Julie Haydon

Contents

Chapter 1
Bees

Fact 1:   Bees are insects.

Insects have three body parts and six legs. Many insects have wings.

Fact 2: There are different kinds of bees.

Bees that make lots of honey are called honeybees.

3

Chapter 2

Honeybees

Fact 3: A honeybee looks like this:

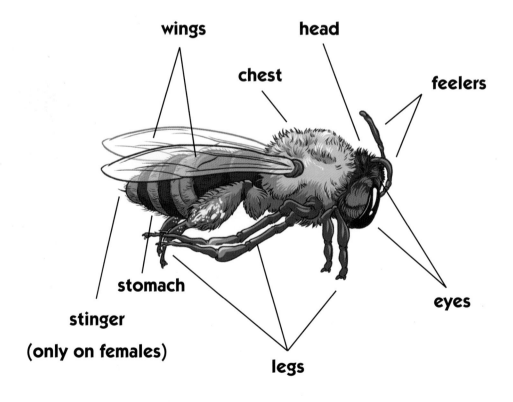

wings

head

chest

feelers

stomach

stinger
(only on females)

legs

eyes

Fact 4:   Honeybees live in many places.

Some honeybees
live in **the wild**.

Some honeybees live on farms.

Chapter 3
Living Together

Fact 5: Honeybees live in **hives**.

Honeybees on farms make their hives
in places made out of wood.
People make these wooden beehives.

Fact 6: Honeybees live in big groups called **colonies**.

A colony is made up of thousands of bees.

Chapter 4
Honey

Fact 7:   Honeybees eat **nectar**.

Nectar is a sweet juice inside flowers. The honeybees fly from flower to flower sucking up the nectar.

They take the nectar from the flowers
to their hive and turn it into honey.
They eat the honey during the winter
when there aren't many flowers.

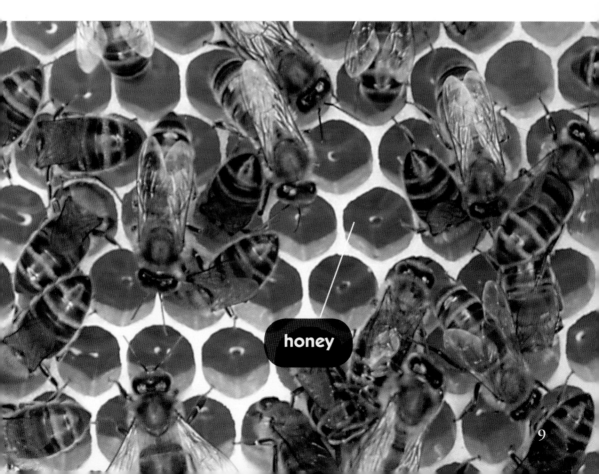

honey

Chapter 5

Pollen

Fact 9: Honeybees pick up **pollen**.

Pollen is a yellow powder inside flowers.
The honeybees put the pollen in little sacks
on the backs of their legs.
The bees take the pollen back to their hive.

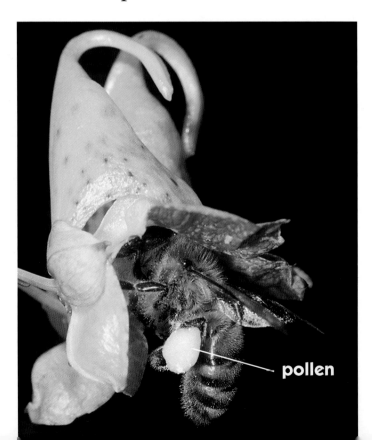

pollen

Fact 10: Honeybees eat pollen.

They give pollen to the baby bees to eat, too.
The pollen helps the baby bees to grow.

baby
bees

Chapter 6
Wax

Fact 11: Honeybees make **wax** inside their bodies.

They use their legs to shape the wax into **honeycombs**.

This is a honeycomb.

Fact 12: Honeycombs are full of six-sided **cells**.

The bees put the honey and pollen in the cells.

cells

Chapter 7

Bee Farming

Fact 13: A bee farmer is called a beekeeper.

Beekeepers wear special clothes
so that the bees cannot sting them.

Fact 14: Some beekeepers keep honeybees for the honey and wax they make.

Some beekeepers sell the honey and wax.

People put honey on bread and on other foods.
People use honey in cooking.

Fact 16: People use wax.

People make candles, crayons, and other things from beeswax.

beeswax

Chapter 8

New Plants

Fact 17: Honeybees help some plants to grow.

Pollen sticks to honeybees.
Some of the pollen falls off the bees
as they fly from flower to flower.
Pollen from one flower falls inside
another flower of the same kind.
This makes seeds grow inside the flower.
New plants grow from the seeds.

Fact 18: Some beekeepers keep honeybees because they help plants on their farm to grow.

Some beekeepers **rent** their honeybees to other farmers so that the bees can help the farmers' plants to grow.

Chapter 9

Jobs for Honeybees

Fact 19: There is one queen bee in a colony.

The queen bee is the leader of the bees.
She lays all the eggs.
She lays the eggs in cells in the honeycomb.
Baby bees come out of the eggs.

queen bee

Fact 20: Most of the bees in a colony are worker bees.

Worker bees are female.
They do most of the work
both in and out of the hive.
They cannot lay eggs.

Drones **mate** with the queen bee.
The queen bee lays her eggs
after she has mated.

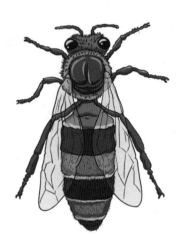

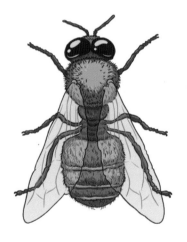

queen bee   drone   worker bee

Chapter 10

Teamwork

Fact 22: Honeybees work in teams.

The bees in a colony need each other.

Glossary

cells	small six-sided openings in the honeycomb
colonies	big groups of honeybees that live and work together
hives	homes for honeybees
honeycombs	structures made of wax inside the hive
mate	when a male and a female join together to make babies
nectar	a sweet juice inside flowers
pollen	a yellow powder inside flowers that is needed to make seeds
rent	when somebody gives a person money to use something that the person owns
the wild	in nature, away from people
wax	a soft substance made inside honeybees that they use to build their honeycombs

Index